A.R. 8.4, MG, Pts. 3

MW01152254

WORLD IN FOCUS
FOCUS ON
ITALY

JEN GREEN

WORLD ALMANAC® LIBRARY

Please visit our web site at: www.garethstevens.com
For a free color catalog describing World Almanac® Library's list of high-quality books
and multimedia programs, call 1-800-848-2928 (USA) or 1-800-387-3178 (Canada).
World Almanac® Library's fax: (414) 332-3567.

Library of Congress Cataloging-in-Publication Data available upon request from publisher.
Fax (414) 336-0157 for the attention of the Publishing Records Department.

Green, Jen.
    Focus on Italy / Jen Green.
       p. cm. — (World in focus)
    Includes bibliographical references and index.
    ISBN-13: 978-0-8368-6736-7 (lib. bdg.)
    ISBN-13: 978-0-8368-6743-5 (softcover)
    1. Italy—Juvenile literature. 2. Italy—Textbooks. I. Title.
  DG417.G68 2007
  945—dc22   2006025094

This North American edition first published in 2007 by
World Almanac® Library
A Member of the WRC Media Family of Companies
330 West Olive Street, Suite 100
Milwaukee, WI 53212 USA

This U.S. edition copyright © 2007 by World Almanac® Library. Original edition copyright © 2006 Wayland.
First published in 2006 by Wayland, an imprint of Hachette Children's Books, 338 Euston Road, London NW1 3BH, U.K.

Commissioning editor: Nicola Edwards
Editor: Patience Coster
Inside design: Chris Halls, www.mindseyedesign.co.uk
Cover design: Hodder Wayland
Series concept and project management by EASI-Educational Resourcing
(info@easi-er.co.uk)
Statistical research: Anna Bowden
Maps and graphs: Martin Darlison, Encompass Graphics

T 22910

World Almanac® Library editor: Alan Wachtel
World Almanac® Library cover design: Scott Krall

Picture acknowledgements:
The author and publisher would like to thank the following for allowing their pictures to be reproduced in this publication:
CORBIS 5 (Massimo Mastrorillo), 10 (Rachel Royse), 11, 13 (Bettmann), 17 (Sergio Pitamitz/zefa), 22 (Enrico Oliverio/
ANSA/epa), 23 (John and Lisa Merrill), 24, 25 (Alberto Pizzoli), 33 (Stephane Cardinale/People Avenue), 35 (Zohra
Bensemra/Reuters), 37 (Bob Krist), 43 (Silvia Morara), 44 (Jodi Hilton), 49 (Sandro Vannini), 53 (Fabio Muzzi/CORBIS
Sygma), 55 (Michael S Yamashita), 59 (Peter Turnley); EASI-Images (Rob Bowden) *title page* and 21, 6, 9, 12, 16, 19, 20, 28,
29, 30, 31, 32, 34, 36, 39, 41, 45, 46, 50, 54, 56; EASI-Images (Ed Parker) 14, 15, 18, 26, 27, 38, 40, 48, 51, 52, 57, 58; Chris
Fairclough Worldwide/Chris Fairclough 4, 8, 42, 47.

The directional arrow portrayed on the map on page 7 provides only an approximation of north.
The data used to produce the graphics and data panels in this title were the latest available at the time of production.

Printed in China

1 2 3 4 5 6 7 8 9 10 09 08 07 06

CONTENTS

Cover: The coast of the town of Vietri sul Mare, south of Naples.

Title page: The main *piazza* at Amalfi, near Naples.

CHAPTER 1

Italy –
An Overview

The shape of Italy is instantly recognizable. The country is made up mainly of a slender, boot-shaped peninsula jutting into the northern Mediterranean Sea, along with two large islands, Sicily and Sardinia. To the north, Italy shares borders with France, Switzerland, Austria, and Slovenia. Italy is about the same size as Arizona. It has a highly successful economy, and, in 2005, it was ranked as the seventh wealthiest economy in the world. Italy's economic strength is partly a result of its strategic position at the center of Europe. As a member of the European Union (EU), Italy's economy is linked with other EU members, such as France and Germany. In 2002, Italy's adoption of the European Union currency—the euro—led to even closer ties with other EU members that had also adopted the euro.

OLD AND NEW

Italy is both an ancient country and a fairly young one. Italian culture has influenced the Mediterranean region for many hundreds of years, yet 150 years ago the unified country called Italy did not exist. Two thousand years ago, Italy was home to one of the ancient world's most advanced civilizations, the Roman Empire. In about A.D. 100, the Romans ruled a vast empire that included many of the lands bordering the Mediterranean Sea.

After the fall of the Roman Empire in the fifth century, Italy was divided into several small

▼ Italy's capital, Rome, includes Vatican City within its borders. St. Peter's Square, shown here, is the heart of Vatican City.

city-states, often ruled by foreign powers. The influence of Italian culture, however, remained strong in Europe and beyond. As the home of the papacy, the city of Rome became the center of western Christianity. Throughout medieval times, the popes wielded great worldly, as well as religious, power. During the fourteenth to sixteenth centuries, the region of Italy found itself at the heart of the great artistic awakening known as the Renaissance. Italian painters, sculptors, poets, and other artists produced great art treasures and writings.

UNIFICATION

In the 1850s, the movement to unify Italy gathered strength. In 1861, the various political regions were brought together as a single country. During the twentieth century, Italy met with mixed fortunes. The country sided with Germany during World War II and suffered a great defeat. During the 1950s, Italy industrialized rapidly and its economy boomed, although its economic progress later slowed.

As citizens of a leading industrial nation, most Italians enjoy a fairly high standard of living. However, a deep divide exists between northern Italy and southern Italy in terms of living standards and resources. Northern Italy is wealthy and more industrialized; southern Italy is poorer and more agricultural. Since the 1950s, successive Italian governments have tried to reduce this divide. These governments have spent large sums of money on improving the resources and industries of the south, but their programs have achieved with varying degrees of success. In the 1990s, political parties campaigning for northern Italy to cut its ties with southern Italy and become more independent gained considerable support among people in the north.

 Did You Know?

Two small, independent countries are located inside Italy's borders: the tiny republic of San Marino, which dates back to A.D. 301, and Vatican City, which lies inside Rome.

◀ Renaissance Italy produced a wealth of great art treasures. This copy of Michelangelo's sculptural masterpiece, *David*, stands outside the Palazzo Vecchio, in Florence. The original statue stands inside the Galleria dell'Accademia, also in Florence.

PEOPLE AND LANGUAGE

About 96 percent of Italy's people are ethnic Italians (including Sardinians, who view the large island of Sardinia as partly separate from mainland Italy). Small numbers of French, Germans, and Slovenes live near Italy's northern borders, while some Albanians and Greeks live in the south of the country. Italian is a Romance language, derived from Latin and based on a dialect spoken in Tuscany in medieval times. In about 1900, only a few of Italy's people spoke what is now standard Italian. Most spoke regional dialects. Today, regional dialects are used mainly by the older generation. Italy's long history as a group of city-states has left Italians with a sense of regional identity that can appear stronger than their sense of national identity. Many people in the country see themselves first as belonging to a particular city or region and second as Italian.

ITALY'S REPUTATION

Italy's historic cities, rich culture, and sunny climate are world renowned. They attract vacationers, and tourism is central to Italy's economy. Italy is also famed as the land of fast cars, high fashion, opera, and romance. The national flair for design ensures that Italian cars, clothes, and other products sell well abroad. The country is also famous for its food. Italian-style foods such as pizza, pasta, and ice cream are eaten all over the world.

Italy is also well known for some less positive aspects of its culture. It is notorious as a base for organized crime—especially that of the international criminal organization known as the Mafia, which is involved in the illegal-drug trade. Since the 1990s, Italy has been rocked by a series of scandals, with accusations of bribery, corruption, and even violence leveled at leading politicians and businessmen. Such accusations are still being made today.

Physical Geography

- Land area: 113,492 sq miles/294,020 sq km
- Water area: 2,783 sq miles/7,210 sq km
- Total area: 116,275 sq miles/301,230 sq km
- World rank (by area): 70
- Land boundaries: 1,200 miles/1,932 km
- Border countries: Austria, France, Vatican City (Holy See), San Marino, Slovenia, Switzerland
- Coastline: 4,723 miles/7,600 km
- Highest point: Monte Bianco de Courmayeur, secondary peak of Mont Blanc (15,578 ft/ 4,748 m)
- Lowest point: Mediterranean Sea (0 ft/0 m)

NB: all the above data includes Sardinia and Sicily
Source: CIA World Factbook

◀ The Italian diet includes plenty of fresh produce, much of which is grown locally. This stall sells fresh citrus juices.

Legend
★ Capital
● Cities > 500,000
● Cities > 200,000
• Cities > 100,000
• other cities
▲ Mountain

CHAPTER 2

History

The first settlements in Italy were created in about 4000 B.C., although human remains have been found in the region dating from 20,000 B.C. During the ninth century B.C., Phoenicians from the North African city of Carthage colonized southern Italy. Later, invaders from Greece claimed much of Italy as part of the Greek Empire. By the seventh century B.C., a people called the Etruscans dominated central Italy and had formed an association of twelve city-states called Etruria.

▼ Gladiator contests and reenactments of sea battles were staged at the Colosseum in Rome (below). Throughout the Roman world, entertainment was staged in amphitheaters like this one.

THE ROMAN EMPIRE

According to legend, Rome was founded in 753 B.C. In 509 B.C., a Latin-speaking people, the Latini, who probably originated north of the Alps, drove the Etruscan king out of Rome and founded the Roman republic. Through a series of wars, the Romans carved out an empire that, by A.D. 100, stretched from Britain east to Syria and south into North Africa. The Romans were skilled architects and engineers and built a network of roads, forts, and towns throughout their empire. They constructed aqueducts to carry water and introduced new farming practices and other innovations that made life easier. Wealthy Romans lived comfortably in town houses or country villas complete with

central heating and sanitation. On large estates and in well-to-do households, slaves did much of the work.

Jesus Christ lived and died in the Roman province of Palestine in the Middle East. During the early centuries A.D., Christianity took hold in the Roman world, replacing other religions. At first, the new religion was outlawed. But in A.D. 313, the Roman emperor Constantine allowed Christians to worship. Rome soon became the base of the papacy. In the third century, the Roman Empire was divided in half to make it easier to run. The western half of the empire was ruled from Rome. The government of the eastern half was based in Byzantium, which later became known as Constantinople and is now Istanbul, Turkey. The Western Empire came under increasing threat from warlike peoples to the north, whom the Romans called Barbarians. In A.D. 476, the Barbarian leader Odoacer sacked Rome and deposed the last emperor. In the east, the Byzantine Empire remained strong.

 Did You Know?

The Romans were responsible for Italy's name. They called the southern part of the country *Italia*, which means "land where oxen graze."

Focus on: Vesuvius and Pompeii

In A.D. 79, Mount Vesuvius, a volcano near the city of Naples, erupted without warning. From nearby, the Roman writer Pliny the Younger saw a large cloud of dark ash rise from the mountain and spread across the sky. The cloud of burning ash engulfed the town of Pompeii, which was located at the foot of Vesuvius. All of the town's inhabitants perished. In the eighteenth century, Pompeii was rediscovered and excavated. The thick layer of ash had preserved the town's streets perfectly. Elaborate mosaics and frescos were found intact in wealthy villas. The imprints of the bodies of Pompeii's citizens and even their pets had also been preserved by the ash.

◀ The Roman town of Pompeii is now a major tourist attraction. Streets, buildings, and even graffiti on walls have been preserved by the volcanic ash which fell on the town almost two thousand years ago.

Following the breakup of the Western Empire, the geographical region of Italy was divided into a number of smaller territories, many of which became parts of other empires. Meanwhile, the popes grew more powerful, and acquired much of central Italy, which became known as the Papal States. Between the ninth and fourteenth centuries, successive popes vied for control of northern Italy. To the north, the Holy Roman Empire ruled much of western Europe. To the south, Byzantium ruled southern Italy. Later, the Arabs, the Normans, and the Spanish ruled southern Italy.

CITY-STATES AND FOREIGN RULE

During the tenth to fourteenth centuries, small, independent city-states arose across much of Italy. Each of these states centered on a city such as Venice, Genoa, Milan, Florence, or Pisa and was governed either by a council of elders or a wealthy merchant or nobleman. City-states such as Milan, Genoa, and Venice grew prosperous through trade and banking, and Venice even established an empire of its own. The rulers of Italian city-states were important patrons of the arts, who supported the great artistic flowering of the Renaissance.

Between 1500 and 1800, much of Italy was ruled by foreign powers such as France, Spain, and Austria. After the French Revolution (1789–1792), the French emperor Napoleon Bonaparte conquered northern Italy and set up a series of

▼ The Norman rulers of Sicily were great builders, and their architectural influence can be seen in the sweeping lines of this cathedral in Palermo. The Normans employed Arabic craftsmen to decorate the interiors with dazzling mosaics.

republics. After Napoleon's defeat in 1815, Italy was returned to its former state, with the north ruled by Austrians, the south by the Spanish, and the center by the Papal States. But Napoleon's occupation of Italy had given many of its people a taste for a unified, independent nation. The independent kingdom of Piedmont and the island of Sardinia became the focus for unification.

? Did You Know?

In about A.D. 1300, approximately four hundred separate city-states flourished in Italy.

▼ A fifteenth-century woodcut of the port of Genoa. This city-state, which was a leading center of trade, was the birthplace of Christopher Columbus.

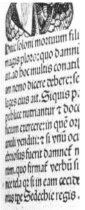

Focus on: Italian Explorers

In medieval times, many great travelers and explorers came from Italy. In the late thirteenth century, Marco Polo, a young Venetian, was one of the first Europeans to visit China. He wrote a famous book about his travels. In 1492, Christopher Columbus, a navigator from Genoa, was commissioned by Spain to sail across the Atlantic. His mission was to reach China and the east, but he reached the "New World" of the Americas instead. Another Italian explorer, Amerigo Vespucci, gave his name to the Americas. In the fifteenth century, the Venetian navigator Giovanni Caboto, known as John Cabot, explored the coast of Canada.

UNIFICATION AND WORLD WAR

In the 1850s, the *Risorgimento*, or the movement to unify the diverse states of Italy, gathered strength. Unification was achieved through the work of three key figures: Giuseppe Mazzini, a political activist; Count Camillo Cavour, chief minister of Piedmont-Sardinia; and Giuseppe Garibaldi, a brilliant soldier. In 1859, Cavour's forces defeated the Austrians in northern Italy.

The army of Piedmont moved south, while Garibaldi invaded Sicily with a force of 1,000 men and swept north. The independent Kingdom of Italy, which was proclaimed in 1861, was soon enlarged by the addition of Venice and the Papal States.

Beginning in the late 1800s, Italy took part in the "scramble for Africa," during which European powers competed to seize African territories. Italy took control of Eritrea, Somalia, and Libya. During World War I, Italy sided with the Allies in an attempt to increase its territory but did not make substantial gains. In the 1920s, the Fascist leader Benito Mussolini rose to power by promising to make Italy a great nation. In 1922, Mussolini's forces marched on Rome, and the king, Victor Emmanuel III, declared Mussolini to be premier of Italy. By 1925, Mussolini had become dictator of Italy.

In 1936, Italy's forces occupied Ethiopia in East Africa. In 1940, Italy entered World War II on the side of Nazi Germany but was defeated by the Allies, who, by 1943, had occupied southern Italy. Italy's government surrendered and overthrew Mussolini, but the Nazis took control and installed Mussolini as head of a puppet state in the north. Italy became a war zone, as Allied forces and Italian partisans—resistance fighters opposed to the Nazis—battled their way north through the country. By 1945, Mussolini had been killed, and the Allies were victorious.

◀ A statue of Italian national hero Giuseppe Garibaldi. Garibaldi's force of 1,000 volunteers were nicknamed "redshirts." In 1860, they conquered Sicily and then Naples.

INTO THE TWENTY-FIRST CENTURY

After the war, much of Italy lay in ruins. However, with the help of the United States, the post-war period was a time of rapid economic growth and industrialization. In 1957, Italy became a founding member of the European Economic Community (EEC). But in the 1960s, Italy's economy slowed and inflation rose.

During the 1970s, the rise in Italy of right-wing and left-wing terrorist groups that were opposed to all political parties brought turmoil to the country. Some of these groups carried out bombings, kidnappings, and murders. In 1978, a left-wing extremist group called the Red Brigades kidnapped and killed a former prime minister, Aldo Moro. The mid-1980s were better times for Italy, with partial economic recovery and the defeat of terrorism. During the 1990s, however, the government of Italy was involved in a series of political scandals, with many politicians accused of criminal activities. Italy's attempts to stamp out organized crime and corruption have continued into the twenty-first century.

▼ Benito Mussolini (left) and Nazi leader Adolf Hitler watch a parade held when the Italian dictator visited Germany in 1937.

CHAPTER 3

Landscape and Climate

With a land area of 113,492 square miles (294,020 square kilometers) , Italy is smaller than France, but larger than Britain. The boot-shaped peninsula of Italy is nowhere more than 106 miles (170 kilometers) wide, but it is 746 miles (1,200 km) long. Italy is surrounded by the seas of the Mediterranean on three sides: the Ligurian Sea, to the northwest; the Adriatic, to the east; the Tyrrhenian Sea, to the west; and the Ionian Sea, to the southeast.

Italy's coastline stretches 4,723 miles (7,600 km). The "toe" of Italy lies close to the island of Sicily, the Mediterranean's largest island which covers 9,924 sq miles (25,709 sq km). The rocky island of Sardinia, occupying 9,298 sq miles (24,089 sq km), lies to the west across the Tyrrhenian Sea. In addition, Italy has more than 3,000 smaller islands, such as Elba and Capri.

MOUNTAINS AND LOWLANDS

Much of Italy is covered by uplands. Located in the country's far north, the Alps are Italy's highest mountains, rising to 15,578 feet (4,748 meters) on the slopes of Mont Blanc, which has its summit in France. The Alps form Italy's borders with France, Switzerland, and Austria. East of the Alps rise the Dolomites, a range of craggy limestone peaks. The Apennines form a rugged mountain crest zigzagging down central Italy for about 839 miles (1,350 km).

Lowlands cover less than one-quarter of Italy. A large lowland belt lies in the country's north, sandwiched between the Alps and the

▼ Snow lingers in the Italian Alps late into summer. The region's glaciers, however, are shrinking because of global warming.

Apennines. In this region, the plain of Lombardy in the west merges with the Po Valley to the east. This area is extensively farmed and densely populated. Other low-lying plains are found along parts of the west coast and in Puglia, which forms Italy's "heel."

Italy's longest river is the Po, which rises in the Alps and flows 405 miles (652 km) to the Adriatic. Other rivers in the country include the Adige, the

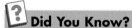

Did You Know?

The word *volcano* comes from the small volcanic island of Vulcano off Italy's southern coast.

Tiber, and the Arno. In the south, some rivers—*fiumare*—dry up in summer. The large, beautiful lakes of Garda, Maggiore, and Como are in Italy's north, while Lake Trasimeno is in central Italy.

Italy lies on a geological fault line, a zone of weakness in Earth's crust. Magma (molten rock) surging up through cracks (faults) in Earth's crust produces volcanic eruptions. Italy's volcanoes include Mount Etna, on Sicily, and the volcanic island of Stromboli. Mount Vesuvius, near Naples, famously erupted in A.D. 79 and, more recently, in 1631 and 1944. Some experts believe another eruption of Vesuvius is due.

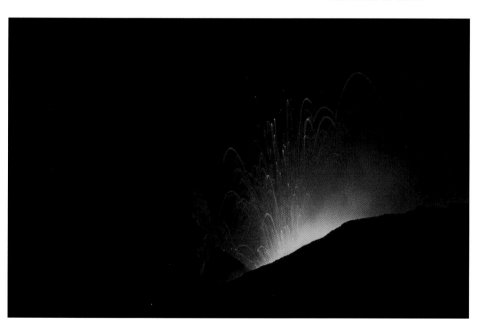

◀ Frequent minor volcanic eruptions shoot from the crater on Mount Stromboli, located on one of the Aeolian islands off the coast of Sicily. Red-hot rocks shoot into the air and fall into the sea with a hissing sound.

Focus on: Where Plates Collide

Italy is located on a border zone where two of the huge tectonic plates that form Earth's crust meet and push together. Millions of years ago, these same plates—the European and African plates—created the Alps, fold mountains which formed as rock crumpled upwards as the plates collided.

The enormous pressure created by the plate collision also causes rocks to shift, sometimes producing violent earthquakes. Central and southern Italy are particularly prone to earthquakes. Italy's last major earthquake was in 2002 and measured 5.9 on the Richter scale.

CLIMATE

Italy is known for its sunny climate, and its skies are mostly clear during spring, summer, and fall. In winter, the country's skies are often overcast and rainy. In spring, hot, dry air from Africa moves north to cover much of Italy. Summers in Italy (June-August) are mainly dry, with occasional thunderstorms. In fall, cool, moist air moves in from the Atlantic Ocean. Winter (December-February) brings the country's coolest temperatures.

The altitude of the land and its closeness to the sea affect local climates and result in cooler uplands and some milder climates near the coast. Because of Italy's long north-south extent, the country's regions vary in climate. These differences are most obvious in winter. Much of the north has a temperate climate, meaning it is

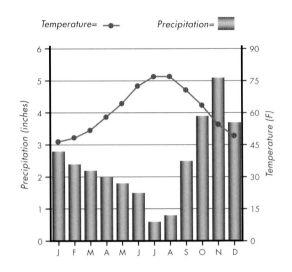

Temperature= ●   Precipitation= ▦

▲ Average monthly climate conditions in Rome

▼ Because of its dry climate, much of southern Italy features scrubby vegetation. This is the coast around the town of Vietri sul Mare, south of Naples.

cooler and wetter than the southern areas. Milan has average minimum temperatures of 34 °F (1 °C) in January. Its temperatures climb to 82 °F (28 °C) in summer. Italy's climate becomes hotter and drier further south. Palermo, on Sicily, has average minimum temperatures of 46 °F (8 °C) in January, but its temperatures soar to 86 °F (30 °C) in summer. Southern Italy is known as the *Mezzogiorno*—the land of the midday sun—because of the scorching heat that occurs at about noon during summers. Parts of the south and center of Italy are extremely dry and prone to drought.

VEGETATION

Italy's regional differences in climate and terrain suit different types of vegetation, making possible the variety of scenery in the country. In the north, the lower slopes of the Alps are clothed in forests of fir and pine, with

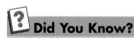

Did You Know?

The climate of southern and central Italy—hot, dry summers and mild winters—is known as a "Mediterranean" climate wherever it occurs around the world.

alpine meadows higher up. Forests of oak, beech, and pine once covered much of Italy, but these were mostly felled long ago for timber and agriculture. Farming has transformed areas such as the Po Valley, and coastal marshlands have been drained for agriculture. Cypress trees dot the rolling hills of Tuscany in the west. Dense, thorny scrubland called *macchia* covers dry, stony terrain in the south and on Sardinia.

Focus on: Natural Disasters

Many natural disasters—including earthquakes, volcanic eruptions, droughts, and floods—have struck Italy. In 1908, the port of Messina, in Sicily, was devastated by a violent earthquake that killed more than 70,000 people. Mount Etna, on Sicily, is one of Europe's highest active volcanic mountains. Major eruptions occurred there in 1996 and in 2002. In 1994, torrential rains in northwest Italy caused extensive flooding that killed about one hundred people.

▼ Tall cypress trees frame a farmhouse on a hilltop in Tuscany, providing protection from cold winter winds.

CHAPTER 4

Population and Settlements

In 2005, over 57 million people lived in Italy. Between 1850 and 1970, Italy's population rose steeply, but since 1995, the figure has remained almost constant. In the 1950s, the country's population increased by about 7 percent each year, but growth fell to less than 4 percent in the 1980s and to zero by the mid-1990s. This so-called zero population growth occurs when numbers of births and deaths are equal, and, therefore, cancel each other out.

By 2005, Italy's population had actually started to fall slightly. Experts predict that this trend will continue over the next decades. Beginning with a population equal in size to that of France and Britain, Italy's population looks set to fall to a similar level to that of Spain today. Average Italian families have only 1.2 children—fewer than the average of 2.05 children needed to keep the population the same size. Some of the reasons for this include the fact that Italians are marrying later and that more Italian women are going out to work before and after marriage. Many families want a lifestyle they could not afford if they had more children. In general, family sizes are larger in the country's south than in its north.

In 2003, just over two-thirds of Italy's people were between 15 and 64 years of age, with only 14 percent under the age of 15. Almost one-fifth of Italians were age 65 and over, with better health care helping people to live longer. This pattern is similar in many European countries. The government fears that in twenty years not enough adults will be working and paying taxes to support the large numbers of older people who need pensions, increased medical care, and other services. Italy's government is now encouraging people to work longer and retire later.

◀ High-rise housing is found in Italy's suburbs and in the centers of its cities. Modern apartment buildings are a common feature. The apartments shown here are located in a suburban area of Rome and were built during the 1960s.

NORTH AND SOUTH

In 2004, Italy had an average population density of about 492 per sq mile (190 people per sq km). The country's population, however, is not evenly distributed. More people live in fertile lowlands and industrial areas, while mountains and dry areas have fewer people. In the nineteenth and twentieth centuries, a marked contrast developed between northern Italy and southern Italy in terms of population and industrial development. Northern Italy became more densely populated, with a climate and terrain favorable for farming, more natural resources, and better developed industries. Fewer people lived in southern Italy, with its harsh climate, poor farms, and less developed industries.

▲ Men enjoy a game of cards at a social club in Sorrento. The proportion of Italy's population aged 65 and over is steadily increasing.

Did You Know?

Many Italians live in palazzos. A palazzo is not a palace, as the Italian word implies, but an apartment building.

Population Data

- Population: 57.3 million
- Population 0–14 yrs: 14%
- Population 15–64 yrs: 67%
- Population 65+ yrs: 19%
- Population growth rate: -0.1%
- Population density: 492.7 per sq mile/ 190.2 per sq km
- Urban population: 67%
- Major cities: Milan 4,007,000
                Naples 2,905,000
                Rome 2,628,000

Source: United Nations and World Bank

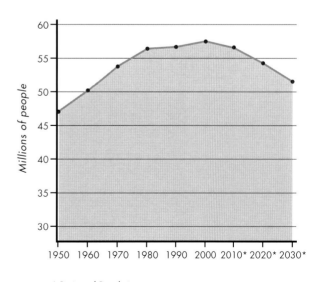

* Projected Population

▲ Population growth, 1950–2030

In the 1950s and 1960s, large numbers of Italians from the south of the country moved to the industrial centers of the north to seek work and a better standard of living. This caused problems such as unemployment and overcrowding in some northern cities, while some villages in the south became deserted. Between 1950 and 1984, Italy's government spent huge amounts of money on the *Cassa per il Mezzogiorno*, a fund to develop the industries, communications, and resources of southern Italy. The fund succeeded in improving transportation, but efforts to relocate industry and business met with mixed results. The south still lags behind the north in natural resources, and its climate is less favorable to farming.

ITALIAN CITIES

Just over two-thirds of Italy's population live in urban areas, a figure that has remained roughly constant since 1995. This figure is low compared with that of many European countries. Beginning in ancient times, settlements grew up in Italy on favored sites such as cool hilltops and fertile river valleys that offered water for irrigation, a means of transportation, and defense against enemies. Unlike most other countries, Italy is not dominated by a single city. Milan, Rome, and Naples are its three largest cities, each with over 2.5 million people. Turin, Bari, Bologna, Florence, Genoa, Catania, Palermo, and Venice are also major metropolitan areas. Each has a distinct character dating from the days of the city-states. For example, the streets of the city of Venice are a system of canals. People travel through the city by boat.

◀ The scene in this narrow backstreet in Naples is typical of many cities in southern Italy.

Towns in Italy are traditionally laid out around one or more squares (*piazze*). Many towns have fine buildings, including churches, dating back to Renaissance, medieval, and even Roman times. Older districts have large, handsome houses built around a central courtyard. In modern suburbs, many people live in apartments in high-rise buildings. The poorest housing is often on the outskirts of towns and cities. Although they have great historical interest, Italian cities are not exempt from problems that plague urban areas the world over, including traffic congestion, overcrowding in poor districts, and pollution.

▶ Every Italian town has at least one *piazza*, although not all towns have one as grand as this one in Amalfi, near Naples.

Focus on: Rome

Rome, called "the eternal city," is Italy's capital and second largest city, after Milan. Its many historic buildings include the Forum, where Romans worshipped and did business, and the Colosseum, where gladiatorial contests were held. Originally built around seven hills at a crossing on the River Tiber, the city is also known for the underground catacombs in which early Christians buried their dead. It is the only city in the world with an independent country inside it—Vatican City. Rome is known for its graceful squares and its fountains dating from about 1600. In the twentieth century, Rome grew rapidly with the construction of many high-rise office and apartment buildings. The city became a thriving center of finance, trade, and industry, including the fashion industry. Modern Rome is a mixture of grand old buildings and modern complexes, with crowded cafés, brightly-lit stores, and noisy traffic that winds through narrow backstreets.

CHAPTER 5

Government and Politics

In 1946, Italians voted to abolish their country's monarchy, and Italy has been a republic ever since. In 1947, the nation's constitution was written to prevent the rise of another dictator like Mussolini. Italy is a parliamentary democracy. Everyone over the age of 18 has the right to vote. The percentage of the population that votes in elections is high compared to many countries. Referendums are sometimes held on major issues, such as abortion and electoral reform.

Italy is divided into twenty administrative regions, each of which has a strong identity. All of these regions have a degree of self-rule and a few, including Sardinia, have considerable autonomy (independence). The regions are subdivided into provinces, and the provinces are divided into units called communes.

ELECTORAL SYSTEM

Italy's parliament, which is based in Rome, has two houses. Italy's electoral system was reformed in 1993. Seventy-five percent of members of both houses are directly elected, with the candidate with the most votes in an area winning the seat and the other parties winning nothing. The remaining 25 percent of members are elected through the system of proportional representation. Using this system, seats are given to parties according to their share of the vote in the whole country. The upper house of Italy's parliament, or Senate, has 315 members, 232 of whom are directly elected and 83 of whom are elected from the regions by proportional representation. The lower house, the Chamber of Deputies, has 630 members, 475 of whom are directly elected and 155 of whom are elected through the system of proportional representation. Senators and deputies serve five-year terms. Italy has relatively few women in parliament compared with some other European countries.

Did You Know?

Voting is considered a civic duty in Italy. Failure to vote in elections is an offense that can lead to a criminal record.

◀ Pope John Paul II addresses Italy's Chamber of Deputies in 2002. Pope John Paul died in 2005 and was succeeded by Pope Benedict XVI.

The president is Italy's head of state, but this position is largely ceremonial. In recent years, however, presidents have taken an active role during times of political turmoil in Italy, such as the period following the scandals of the 1990s. Presidents serve a seven-year term. The prime minister, who is the leader of the most powerful party in Italy's government, chooses the cabinet of ministers. Prime ministers do not serve a fixed term, and Italy is famous for its frequent changes of prime minister and cabinet. Many ministers serve under successive prime ministers, giving continuity to the country's government.

▼ The town hall and main square of Cortona, in Tuscany, is the seat of local government.

POST-WAR POLITICS

Since World War II, Italy's complex electoral system has resulted in governments being formed through coalitions, meaning that a number of political parties has shared power. From 1948 to the mid-1990s, the center-right Christian Democrat Party, which has a broadly conservative outlook, dominated Italian politics. The Christian Democrats formed coalitions with parties that had other views, including socialists and liberals, but kept the Communist Party out of Italy's government, in spite of the fact that it had considerable support.

? Did you know?

Since World War II, few Italian governments have lasted much more than a year.

Since the 1950s, successive governments have steered Italy's economy while trying to tackle persistent problems, including inflation, unemployment, and the organized crime of the Mafia. The division between northern Italy and southern Italy has remained a difficult and lasting issue. During the 1990s, a political party called the *Lega Lombardia* (Northern League) gained support in the north. This group wants the north to become more independent of the south—or even to become a separate country—and to stop subsidizing the south.

CORRUPTION CHARGES

During the early 1990s, a political crisis took place in Italy that changed the face of the country's politics. In 1992, investigations of party finances uncovered a web of bribery and corruption that reached the highest levels of government. Businessmen and politicians from every major party were accused of criminal dealings with the Mafia. The best known of these was Giulio Andreotti, a leading Christian Democrat who had been prime minister six

times. The scandals were called *Tangentopoli*—*tangente* meaning bribe and *poli* meaning city.

Following these scandals, the public lost confidence in existing political parties, and new political alliances were formed. In 1994, the election was won by the center-right Alliance for Freedom, which included the *Forza Italia* (Come on, Italy) Party, led by Silvio Berlusconi, head of the media empire Fininvest. However, Berlusconi was soon forced to resign following accusations of corruption. His departure enabled the center-left Olive Tree Alliance to take power in the late 1990s. In spite of this, Berlusconi was re-elected in 2001. Italy's general election of April 2006 resulted in victory for the Union, a center-left party led by Romano Prodi, who replaced Berlusconi.

▼ Former prime minister Giulio Andreotti (center), was implicated in the *Tangentopoli* scandals of 1992–1993. He is seen here after being tried and acquitted on the charge that he protected the Mafia while he was prime minister.

Focus on: The Mafia

The Mafia is a criminal organization with worldwide connections, including links in the United States. It dates back to medieval times in Sicily, where it grew as a secret organization with the aim of overthrowing foreign rule. Members of the Mafia (*mafiosi*) are bound by a code of silence (*omertà*), which forbids them to betray other *mafiosi*, even rival groups, to the police. By the early twentieth century, the Mafia controlled much of southern Italy. Mussolini almost broke the Mafia's power by imprisoning many of its leaders, but the organization regained strength following World War II, when it became increasingly involved in the illegal-drug trade.

Over the years, Mafia members have carried out assassinations of police officers and judges. Mafia killings include those of the Sicilian anti-Mafia judge Giovanni Falcone and his colleague Paolo Borsellino in 1992. In Italy, the Mafia is known as *la piovra*, or the octopus, because its tentacles reach everywhere. In spite of this, public disgust at Mafia killings and threats has been shown more openly in recent times. Since the 1990s, the police have also scored notable successes in arresting a number of Mafia leaders, including Salvatore Riina (arrested in 1993), Leoluca Bagarella (1995), Giovanni Brusca (1996), Vito Vitale (1998), and Mariano Trioa (2006).

▲ In May 1992, a large crowd attended the funeral of murdered judge Giovanni Falcone in Palermo, Sicily, to show support for Falcone's anti-Mafia stance.

CHAPTER 6

Energy and Resources

Italy's natural resources include fish in its surrounding waters, minerals, forests, and farmland. Its energy resources, however, are fairly scarce, and this has restricted the growth of industry and profits from manufacturing in the country.

ENERGY RESOURCES AND USE

Italy has limited reserves of fossil fuels, including oil, natural gas, and lignite coal. Oil and natural gas are pumped in the Po Valley, Calabria, Sicily, and offshore in the south. Nuclear power provides a relatively small amount of the country's energy. This form of energy is mainly undeveloped as a result of a 1987 referendum in which Italians voted against the construction of more nuclear plants. Public opposition to nuclear power deepened following an accident in 1986 at the Chernobyl nuclear reactor in Ukraine. In terms of renewable energy sources, Italy's hydroelectric power (HEP) potential is well developed. Hydroelectric plants in the Alps and the Apennines harness the energy of fast-flowing streams to provide power for cities and industry. One of the world's first geothermal plants was built at Larderello. In this plant, cold water pumped underground is heated by volcanic rocks and used to produce steam that drives turbines to generate electricity. Italy's use of solar power is limited at present, but, with the country's sunny climate, this form of energy has considerable potential. Italy has one of the fastest growing wind-power industries in the world, and wind and wave power may be utilized more extensively in future.

In 1999, Italy consumed 1.7 percent of all the energy used worldwide. Nearly one-third of this was used in transportation; homes consumed about one-quarter; and industry used one-third. Italy's energy sources do not meet its power needs. About 75 percent of the energy the country uses is imported, mostly in the form of oil and natural gas. The nation's power plants burn oil imported from Libya, Iran, and other oil-producing nations.

◄ In mountainous parts of Italy, hydroelectric plants are used to generate electricity. About 17 percent of Italy's electricity is produced by HEP.

Energy Data

- Energy consumption as % of world total: 1.7%
- Energy consumption by sector (% of total):
  Industry: 31.7
  Transportation: 32.2
  Agriculture: 2.4
  Services: 3.5
  Residential: 26.9
  Other: 3.3
- CO_2 emissions as % of world total: 1.8
- CO_2 emissions per capita in ton per year.: 8

Source: World Resources Institute

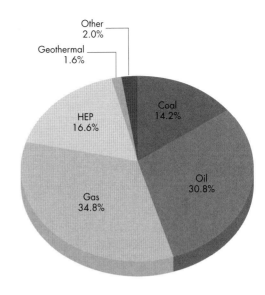

▲ Electricity production by type

Focus on: Carrara Marble

The town of Carrara, located in the Apennines in Tuscany, produces top quality marble for use in construction and sculpture. Mining began in this area in Roman times. Marble, a hard, attractively veined rock, is formed from limestone that has been subjected to great heat and pressure underground. In Renaissance times, the sculptor

Michelangelo came to Carrara to choose the marble he needed for his magnificent sculptures. He carved one of his masterpieces, the statue *David*, from a block of Carrara marble that had been botched and left abandoned by another sculptor. Carrara marble, which can be polished to a smooth, shiny finish, is still prized by sculptors.

◀ Large blocks of fine marble stand ready to be transported from a quarry in Carrara. This marble is traditionally used in sculpture, but it is also in demand in the construction industry.

▲ Salt is extracted from seawater at a plant near Bari. In plants of this type, water is allowed to flood shallow lakes such as the one shown above. The water evaporates, leaving salt deposits behind. The salt is then raked into heaps.

MINERALS

Italy's stocks of minerals are also fairly modest. Sicily, Sardinia, Tuscany, Lombardy, and Piedmont are the chief mining areas. Iron ore, mercury, potash, zinc, lead, feldspar, pumice, and barite are mined commercially. Pyrite from volcanic areas in the south is used in the chemical industry and to produce fertilizer and matches. The quarries of Carrara in Tuscany are famous for their marble. Elsewhere in the country, granite is quarried. Salt is extracted from seawater on the Adriatic coast near Bari. With its limited mineral reserves, Italy must import large quantities of iron ore and other materials it needs for industry.

FISHING, FORESTS, AND FARMLAND

Italy's long coastline is excellent for fishing, a traditional industry in Italy. The waters of the Adriatic and the shallow seas off Sicily provide the country's best fishing grounds. Tuna, sardines, swordfish, and anchovies are among the main species caught commercially. In recent decades, long, floating drift nets have been set to catch fish that swim close to the surface. These nets are so effective that stocks of fish have fallen sharply. The authorities have had to introduce quotas to control the number of fish that can be caught. Shellfish such as shrimp and mussels are also caught, as are squid and octopuses. Fish and shellfish catches are consumed locally by Italians and by tourists. They are also canned or otherwise processed for sale abroad. Fish and shellfish have been raised in shallow lagoons along Italy's coast since Roman times. Today, the main species farmed commercially is the Mediterranean mussel.

After many centuries of felling, there is little forest left in Italy. The country's largest surviving forests grow in Abruzzi, in central Italy, and in Calabria and Puglia, in the south. Native species in these forests include Aleppo and Corsican pines, holm oak, and beech.

About 53 percent of Italy is used for agriculture, with 15 percent used for pasture and 38 percent for crops. This farmland includes 10,414 sq miles (26,980 sq km) of irrigated land. The country's largest tracts of farmland lie in the north. In the Lombardy Plain and the Po Valley, wheat, grapes, olives, and sugar beets are grown. Beef and dairy cattle, pigs, chickens, and sheep are also raised in many parts of Italy. Italy does not, however, produce enough meat to meet its needs and must, for example, import beef from Argentina. The dry climate, poor, stony soil, and steep terrain of southern Italy hinder farming, but sheep and goats are pastured there. Durum wheat is also grown in the south. Terracing on the steep hillsides helps to prevent erosion.

? Did You Know?

The *mattanza* is an annual event in Sicily during which fishermen spread nets in the shallows to catch large, meaty tuna as they arrive to spawn.

▼ Farmers use machines to harvest durum wheat in fields near Foggia, in Puglia. This type of hard wheat is used to make pasta, which is a staple food in Italy.

CHAPTER 7

Economy and Income

Since the 1950s, Italy has shifted from a largely agricultural to a highly industrialized economy. During the 1950s, Italy's economy grew rapidly, but it slowed during the 1960s. Despite some revival between 1970 and 2000, Italy's economic growth now stands at zero. In 2004, Italy had a workforce of 24.27 million, with unemployment estimated at 8.6 percent, and the country ranked seventh in the world in terms of Gross National Income (GNI).

Italy is a leading producer of vehicles, clothing, machinery, iron and steel, chemicals, processed foods, and ceramics. One reason for Italy's economic success since World War II has been its ability to combine new technology with a flair for design across a wide range of manufactured goods, from cars and computers to clothing and kettles.

WORKING CONDITIONS

Many Italian companies are small, family-run businesses employing fewer than one hundred

Focus on: FIAT

The car manufacturer FIAT is one of Italy's most successful companies and a major employer. In 1995, the company employed 145,000 people in Italy alone. It was founded in 1899, at the dawn of the automobile age. Based in Turin, the company now has factories elsewhere in Italy and in 50 countries worldwide. FIAT also owns vehicle manufacturers Lancia, Ferrari, Alfa Romeo, and Maserati, which operate under their own names. In addition to cars, trucks, and tractors, FIAT also makes telecommunications equipment, aircraft engines, and heart pacemakers. The company is also involved in insurance and publishing, owning one of Italy's best-selling newspapers, *La Stampa*.

 Did You Know?

FIAT stands for *Fabbrica Italiana Automobile Torino*—the Italian Automobile Factory of Turin.

◀ Ports such as Castellammare di Stabia, located in the Bay of Naples, have extensive shipyards. These yards were developed by the French occupiers in the eighteenth century and have been in use ever since.

people. However, Italy also has large companies, many of which are part-owned by the government. These include banks, steelworks, shipyards, and car factories. In the second half of the twentieth century, the percentage of women in the country's workforce rose steadily, with large numbers of women working within service industries but fewer working in industry. Italy's wages are relatively low compared with other European nations—another reason why Italy has the edge over some of its competitors.

Unions are strong in Italy. Workers pay high taxes, but working conditions are generally good and pensions generous. A number of small businesses, however, operate within the country's "hidden economy." This means they fail to register and, thus, avoid paying taxes. These businesses tend to pay low wages. Despite attempts to equalize industry and job opportunities throughout Italy, wages in the south lag behind those of the north, and unemployment is higher in the south than in the north.

SERVICE INDUSTRIES AND AGRICULTURE

Service industries make up the most important sector of Italy's economy, employing 65 percent of all of the country's workers and producing 69 percent of its GNI in 2004. The service sector includes jobs in government, trade, finance, transportation, and social services. The tourist industry is geared towards foreign and Italian vacationers. Retail stores, hotels, and restaurants—boosted by tourism—are also major money-earners.

▲ Tourism is an important source of income in beautiful areas of Italy, such as the island of Capri. Boat excursions are popular in many resorts.

Economic Data

- 📁 Gross National Income (GNI) in U.S.$: 1,503,562,000,000
- 📁 World rank by GNI: 7
- 📁 GNI per capita in U.S.$: 26,120
- 📁 World rank by GNI per capita: 26
- 📁 Economic growth: 0%

Source: World Bank

During the 1950s, about 33 percent of all of Italy's workers were involved in agriculture. By 2004, only 5.5 percent of its workers were employed in agriculture, which produced just 3 percent of the GNI. Italy's main crops include wheat, corn, rice, sugar beets, olives, and grapes for winemaking. Many regions of Italy are known for their wines, with climates and soils suiting different grapes. Italy is the world's leading producer of tomatoes and tomato products. Fruits and vegetables grown in Italy include cherries, apples, peaches, oranges, potatoes, soybeans, and globe artichokes.

INDUSTRY AND MANUFACTURING

In 2004, Italy's industrial sector, which includes manufacturing, construction, and mining, employed 29.5 percent of the country's workers and yielded 28 percent of its GNI. In spite of the government's attempt to kick-start manufacturing in the south, Italy's industrial heartland remains the north, particularly in and around the cities of Turin, Milan, and Genoa. The country's craft industries— which produce leather goods, glass, and ceramics—date back to medieval times. Different Italian cities are known for characteristic products, such as leather from Naples, jewelry from Florence, and glass from the island of Murano, in Venice.

Italy is a leader in the world of fashion, producing clothing, shoes, perfume, and accessories. Since the 1950s, top manufacturers have employed cutting-edge designers to create functional but stylish goods, including furniture and tableware. Italy is also a top vehicle manufacturer, with FIAT known for family cars; Ferrari, Alfa Romeo, and Lamborghini for sports and racing cars; Vespa for scooters; and Ducati for motorcycles. Italy also produces aircraft and vehicle parts, including tires by Pirelli. Electronic goods, such as computers, are manufactured in Italy, notably by Olivetti. Zanussi, Delonghi, and others produce domestic appliances, such as refrigerators, stoves, and washing machines.

◄ Many Italians prefer to buy fruits and vegetables from market stalls or small, family-run grocery stores rather than large supermarket chains. This small grocery store is in Sorrento.

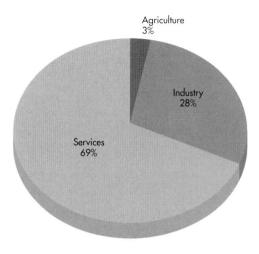

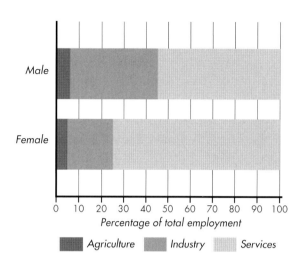

▲ Contribution by sector to national income

▲ Labor force by sector and gender

Focus on: Fashion

Italy is one of the world's fashion capitals, with Italian designers' names such as Gucci, Armani, Prada, Versace, and Benetton known around the world. The fashion industry is mainly based in Milan. Italian people have a reputation for being very fashion conscious, with northern Italians in particular known for their love of designer clothes. Benetton began as a small, family-run business in 1965 and now owns a chain of shops worldwide. Armani, founded in 1975, produces designer clothing, as well as perfume and accessories. Twice yearly, fashion companies launch their new collections on the catwalks of Milan, Paris, London, and New York.

◀ Top models show off the latest collection by Italian designer Donatella Versace at a fashion show in Milan.

CHAPTER 8

Global Connections

Beginning in medieval times, Italian city-states forged links with other European nations through trade and finance. Political links were also made: parts of Italy became colonies of foreign nations such as France, Austria, and Spain. In the early 1900s, Italy itself colonized Somalia, Eritrea, Libya, and Ethiopia. This forged new connections, some of which still influence modern trade patterns. Libya, for example, supplies Italy with oil.

ECONOMIC AND POLITICAL TIES

In 1957, Italy was among the six founding members of the European Economic Community (EEC). The EEC's main purpose was to ease trade among its European members by removing import and export duties. In 1993, the EEC was renamed the European Union (EU). By this time, the group had fifteen member countries. In 2004, it expanded again, to twenty-five members. In addition to enjoying free trade, EU members work for closer political ties. However, Italy, along with most other EU countries, has stopped short of adopting the European constitution, which would represent a further step on the road to union.

EU money has helped to regenerate industry in southern Italy, for example, by providing grants for poor farmers. As EU citizens, Italians are now free to work anywhere within the EU. In 2002, Italy abandoned its national currency, the

▼ Goods are unloaded from a cargo vessel at a major cargo port in Salerno, in southern Italy.

lira, in favor of the single European currency, the euro. Many Italians believe that economic goals set by the EU have forced Italy's government to take a more disciplined approach to the economy. This approach has helped to keep inflation and interest rates low. The euro, however, is not popular with everyone in Italy— partly because prices rose when the euro was adopted—and recently there have been calls to bring back the lira.

Italy is a member of many other international organizations besides the EU. They include the United Nations (UN) and NATO (the North Atlantic Treaty Organization). In the early 2000s, Italy has worked closely with other UN and NATO members to maintain international peace and security following the rise of Islamic terrorism and the terrorist attacks of September 11, 2001.

▲ Italian troops were among the forces involved in the war in Iraq in 2003. Here, two Italian soldiers walk in front of a military police base that has been destroyed by a suicide-bomb attack.

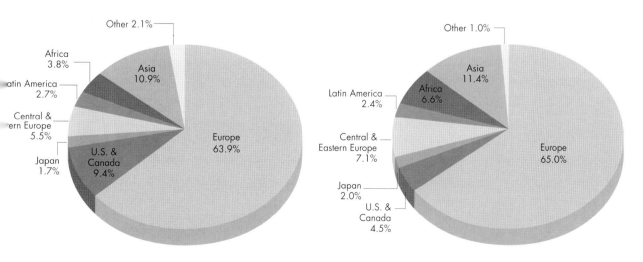

▲ Destination of exports by major trading region   ▲ Origin of imports by major trading region

▲ The Italian obsession with coffee is famous. Italian-style coffee shops have opened in many parts of the world. The coffee shop shown here is in South Korea.

TRADING PARTNERS

Much of Italy's trade is done within Europe, with 63.9 percent of its exports and 65 percent of its imports passing to and from other EU members. Trade with the United States is also important to Italy. The country's main exports are machinery and equipment, food and drink, clothing, shoes, vehicles, and chemicals. Italy's chief imports are machinery, oil, vehicles, chemicals, minerals, and food. Its imports chiefly come from Germany, France, Britain, the Netherlands, and the United States.

Since the 1980s, Italy has spent more on its imports than it has made from its exports, resulting in a trade deficit. The country's trade deficit has also been caused by the rising price of oil, which Italy imports to provide energy. Foreign currency from the tourist industry helps to offset the imbalance.

Italy's trade connections include those of the Mafia, which has unofficial links in other nations in the smuggling and trafficking in illegal drugs. In recent years, the Italy's government has tried to crack down on the "informal sector," which can involve all sorts of activities, from unlicensed but otherwise legal street trading to international drug trafficking. The taxes raised from bringing legal informal businesses within the formal sector would make a substantial contribution to the economy.

 Did You Know?

Between 1861 and 1973, about 26 million Italians emigrated to other countries.

EMIGRATION AND IMMIGRATION

Since the unification of Italy in the 1860s, millions of Italians have emigrated to other countries, including Germany, Switzerland, and the United States. Italians, especially from the country's south, have left in search of work and a better life. In the early 1900s, a huge number of Italians settled in New York City and Boston. Many Italian emigrants also settled in Latin American countries such as Argentina and Brazil. Emigration peaked in the 1950s and 1960s, with 390,000 leaving in 1961 alone.

In the early 1970s, more people immigrated to Italy than emigrated from the country. Some of the arriving immigrants were Italians returning home after having made money abroad. Others were from Eastern Europe and North Africa, where living standards were lower than in Italy. Like other nations, Italy sets quotas to limit the number of immigrants allowed to enter the country legally. Nonetheless, many refugees from nations bordering the Mediterranean take advantage of Italy's long coastline to enter the country illegally. In 1990–1991 and in 1997, waves of Albanian refugees fled to Italy to escape political crisis or war. In 1992 , a flood of refugees from the former Yugoslavia—fleeing war—arrived in Italy.

◀ Italian-American communities in the United States celebrate traditional Catholic feast days. In this picture, Italian-Americans in Manhattan celebrate the feast of San Gennaro.

Focus on: Italian-American Communities

New York, Boston, and many other U.S. cities have Italian neighborhoods. These are the legacy of the early 1900s, when large numbers of Italian immigrants began a new life in the United States. Such neighborhoods have stores selling Italian foods. Many of these neighborhoods also have Italian societies and Catholic church services held in Italian. First-generation Italian immigrants spoke little English, but their children learned English in school. Many third- and fourth-generation Italian-Americans speak very little Italian but still keep strong ties to Italian culture.

CHAPTER 9

Transportation and Communications

Italy's long, narrow shape and mountainous terrain make land travel in the country hard. Sicily, Sardinia, and Italy's smaller islands are, of course, isolated by sea. Nevertheless, Italy's transportation and communications networks are well developed and generally efficient. Between the 1950s and the mid-1980s, the *Cassa per il Mezzogiorno* improved transportation and communications in southern Italy.

ROAD AND RAIL

Italy's 298,078 miles (479,688 km) of roads are all paved, and include 4,312 miles (6,940 km) of *autostrada*, or highways. Between 1955 and 1975, a major road-building program was carried out in Italy largely by private companies, so road users are charged tolls on certain roads. Routes such as the Simplon Pass and the Mont Blanc Tunnel cut through the Alps and link Italy with France, Switzerland, and Austria to the north. The *Autostrada del Sol* (Highway of the Sun) links northern Italy and southern Italy.

? Did You Know?

In 1924, Italy began building the world's first toll highway. This highway linked Milan with Varese, a city north of Milan.

▼ High-speed trains in Italy provide fast connections between cities such as Milan and Rome.

With about one out of every two Italians owning a car, Italy's city roads are congested during rush hours. Overpasses ease congestion, while noisy scooters and small cars navigate narrow streets. Many Italians use public transportation, such as buses, trains, or streetcars. Rome and Milan have subways.

Italian railways are state-owned, subsidized, and inexpensive to use. They run frequently, and many people consider them the best way to travel around Italy. The rail network includes 12,005 miles (19,319 km) of track, of which about 7,457 miles (12,000 km) are electrified. Under Mussolini, the network was improved and magnificent train stations, such as the one in Milan, were built. High-speed trains can cover the 820 miles (1,320 km) from Milan to Reggio di Calabria in eleven hours. Italy's trains, however, are notorious for not being on time, and many journeys involve long delays.

AIR AND WATER TRANSPORTATION

Historically, the sea offered an effective means of travel between Italy's coastal cities. Although it is not as speedy as land travel, sea transportation is still used extensively in Italy. The country has fifteen major seaports, including Genoa; Trieste; Naples; Bari; and Augusta, in Sicily. Many oil tankers dock at Porto Foxi, in Sardinia, or in Genoa. La Spezia, located in Italy's northwest, is mainly a container port.

▶ Electric buses provide efficient transportation in city centers. The bus shown here is in Naples.

Transport & Communications Data

- 🗁 Total roads: 298,078 miles/479,688 km
- 🗁 Total paved roads: 298,078 miles/ 479,688 km
- 🗁 Total unpaved roads: 0 miles/0 km
- 🗁 Total railways: 12,005 miles/19,319 km
- 🗁 Airports: 134
- 🗁 Cars per 1,000 people: 542
- 🗁 Cellular phones per 1,000 people: 1,018
- 🗁 Personal computers per 1,000 people: 231
- 🗁 Internet users per 1,000 people: 337

Sources: World Bank and CIA World Factbook

Ferries and hydrofoils link the mainland with offshore islands and with France, Greece, and Turkey. The Po is Italy's only major navigable river, with canals leading to the northern lakes. The only means of travel within the city of Venice is by water or on foot.

Air travel is the quickest way of covering long distances on the Italian peninsula. Of the 134 airports listed in 2004, over one hundred have paved runways. All of Italy's major cities have airports, with many operating international flights. Leonard da Vinci Airport at Fiumicino, near Rome, and Linate and Malpensa, near Milan, are Italy's busiest airports. The national airline, Alitalia, is largely government owned.

COMMUNICATIONS AND MEDIA

Italy has highly developed communications systems, with fast, fully automated telephone, fax, and data services. In 2003, the country had 26.6 million land telephones. Cellular phone use has risen rapidly since 1995, when only a small

Focus on: Transportation in Venice

With no roads, railways, or subways in Venice, the only way to get around is by boat or on foot. This famous city was founded in the fifth century and lies just offshore in the northeast of the country. It is made up of 117 islands linked by 400 bridges and was originally built on wooden stilts driven into the mud. Venice's "streets" are 150 canals. People travel about the city by *vaporetto* (water bus) or *motoscafo* (launch). Tourists take expensive rides in Venice's famous gondolas. Specific types of gondolas are also used for collecting trash, delivering goods, and funerals.

◀ In Venice, gondolas and other types of boat traffic dock at piers like this one. This view of the Church of Santa Maria della Salute is a favorite of artists and photographers.

percentage of Italians had cell phones; now Italy has one cell phone per person. Internet use is increasing quickly in Italy, although its number of Internet hosts—1.25 million in 2005—is fairly low for a nation with advanced technology. Although only one out of five Italians owned a personal computer in 2002, at least one-third of the population used the Internet.

Italy's state broadcasting company, RAI, has three channels which tend to represent different political viewpoints. Silvio Berlusconi's media empire, Fininvest, operates three more channels, including the popular Canale 5. In addition to three state-run radio stations, Italy has thousands of local and privately owned stations. Half of all Italians own a TV, and the country has one radio per person. Seventy daily newspapers are published in Italy. Owned either by political parties, large businesses, or the Church, many

of them offer a particular political outlook. The most popular daily newspapers are Rome's *La Repubblica*, Milan's *Corriere della Sera*, and Turin's *La Stampa*. Italy also has numerous magazines, mostly dedicated to particular interests, such as sports and fashion.

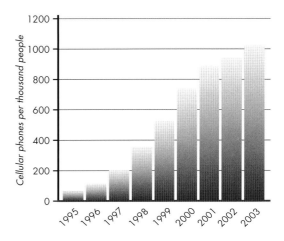

▲ Cellular phone use, 1995–2003

Focus on: Pioneers of Telecommunications

In the early days of telecommunications, Italians led the way with many pioneering inventions. In the 1850s, Giovanni Caselli invented the *pantelegrafo*, a device that was a forerunner of modern fax machines. In 1871, Antonio Meucci designed an early telephone (although, later in the decade, Alexander Graham Bell patented the invention). Guglielmo Marconi was the pioneer of radio who sent the first radio signals across the Atlantic, from Newfoundland to Britain.

◄ Cellular phones are particularly popular with younger people in Italy.

CHAPTER 10

Education and Health

Education and, especially, health are high priorities in Italy. In 2002, Italy spent 4.7 percent of its Gross Domestic Product (GDP) on education. It spent 8.5 percent of its GDP on health—a proportion higher than that spent by Britain but lower than that of the United States.

About 98.5 percent of Italians over the age of fifteen can read and write. Literacy is slightly higher among men than women, reflecting past attitudes to gender and schooling. In the past, more boys than girls continued in secondary education, but this is no longer the case.

PRIMARY AND SECONDARY EDUCATION

In Italy, education is free and compulsory for all children between the ages of 6 and 14. Many children go to nursery school between the ages of 3 and 5. Ninety percent of children go to state-run schools. Compulsory education is split into five years of primary education and three years of middle school (*scuola media*). This may be followed by four or five years of optional senior secondary education, such as study at a technical or teacher-training school or an arts- or science-oriented course at a *liceo*, or college. Italy's education system is currently being overhauled to bring it into line with other EU countries. These changes will extend the age of free, compulsory education to 16. In 2002, 100 percent of Italy's children attended primary school and 88 percent attended secondary school. Forty-one percent of students continued their studies at college or university.

▼ A lesson in progress in a class at a primary school in Rome.

Class sizes are small in Italy. In 2001, there was one teacher for every 10.8 primary school pupils. The school day is fairly short, with classes from about 8:00 A.M. to 2:00 P.M. Italy's school year runs from September to June. Pupils who get poor grades must repeat a year before advancing to a higher level. This affects about 11 percent of girls and more than 20 percent of boys.

HIGHER EDUCATION

Senior secondary school graduates may attend universities, but some programs are so popular that students who want to take them must take an entrance exam. Italy has forty-five public universities. Rome has one with over 170,000 students. The country also has private universities, many of which are run by the Catholic Church. University enrollment has risen steadily since the 1960s, with 1.25 million students now in higher education each year.

Did You Know?

The University of Bologna, located in north-central Italy, is among the world's oldest universities, dating from the eleventh century.

Focus on: The National Curriculum

Italy has introduced a national curriculum to standardize education across the country and ensure all students are well prepared for exams. The government's Ministry of Education is responsible for setting educational priorities and selecting textbooks. Middle school pupils study geography, mathematics, science, history and civic education, Italian, art, and a foreign language. Senior secondary school students follow either an arts-, classics-, language-, or science-based program or a vocational training program, such as teacher-training.

Education and Health

- Life expectancy at birth male: 76.9
- Life expectancy at birth female: 82.9
- Infant mortality rate per 1,000: 4
- Under five mortality rate per 1,000: 4
- Physicians per 1,000 people: 6.1
- Health expenditure as % of GDP: 8.5%
- Education expenditure as % of GDP: 4.7%
- Primary school net enrollment: 100%
- Student-teacher ratio, primary: 10.8
- Adult literacy as % age 15+: 98.5

Source: United Nations Agencies and World Bank

◀ Chinese students at Bologna University, one of Europe's oldest centers of learning.

University tuition in Italy is quite low. Students do not, however, receive grants to pay for living expenses. Many Italian university students live with their parents to avoid paying rent. Many also work part-time to cover their living expenses, which means they take longer to complete their degrees. Since the 1960s, the number of Italian women in higher education has risen steadily, but unemployment is higher among female graduates than among males.

HEALTH

Standards of medical care in Italy are generally good. The country's national health plan provides low-cost medical care for all citizens. With one doctor for every 227 patients, Italy has a high doctor-to-patient ratio. Most Italians eat a healthy diet, including plenty of fresh fruit and vegetables. Pasta is central to the Italian diet. In general, Italians eat fewer processed foods that are high in fat and sugar than people in many other Western countries.

Infant mortality is low in Italy, with just 4 deaths out of every 1,000 live births in 2003. The death rate for children under five is also low, with 4 deaths out of every 1,000 children. Life expectancy at birth rose steadily in Italy in the late twentieth century as a result of improvements in public health and sanitation and continuing advances in medicine. In 1960, Italy's average life expectancy at birth was 69.1 years, rising to 73.9 in 1980, and to 79.8 in 2003. As is the case elsewhere in the world, women

▼ A doctor examines an elderly patient at the patient's home in Basilicata, a poor part of southern Italy.

generally live longer than men. Average life expectancy in Italy in 2003 was 82.9 years for women and 76.9 years for men.

As more people live longer, the increasing number of older people puts more and more pressure on Italy's health care system. Changes are being made in the country to cope with the growing demands from older people. In the past, older people in Italy were usually cared for by their families, but as more women are working outside the home, this is changing.

The major causes of death in Italy are cancer and heart disease. In 2005, there were an estimated 10.3 deaths for every 1,000 people—similar to other nations in Western Europe. The number of deaths per thousand in Italy

actually rose slightly in the 1990s, but has since fallen. HIV/AIDS affected an estimated 0.5 percent of Italy's population in 2005. About 100 people in Italy died of AIDS in 2003.

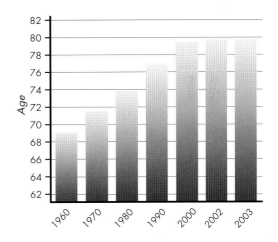

▲ Life expectancy at birth, 1960–2003

▲ The Italian diet consists of a relatively healthy balance of fresh foods, including meats, which provide protein, and carbohydrates such as pasta and bread. Italians also eat lots of fresh vegetables and salads.

CHAPTER 11

Culture and Religion

Italy is internationally known for its great artistic achievements, particularly those dating from the Renaissance but also many from modern times. As the home of the pope, it is the spiritual heartland of Roman Catholics throughout the world.

ART AND LITERATURE

Renaissance means rebirth. During this era—from the fourteenth to the sixteenth centuries—classical arts and learning were revived and new art forms evolved. Great Renaissance artists include Giotto (ca. 1267–1337), Sandro Botticelli (1444–1510), and Raphael (1483–1520). Michelangelo (1475–1564) was a Florentine sculptor, painter, architect, and poet. His sculpture *David* and his frescos in the Sistine Chapel in Rome are masterpieces of the depiction of the human form. Another great Italian artist, Leonardo da Vinci (1452–1519), produced one of the world's most famous paintings, the *Mona Lisa*. Leonardo was also a great scientist and engineer. Some of Italy's best-known writers also date from Renaissance times. Dante (1265–1321), Petrarch (1304–1374), and Giovanni Boccaccio (1313–1375) all produced great works of poetry. These include Dante's epic poem *The Divine Comedy*, which describes a journey through hell and purgatory to heaven, and *The Decameron*, a collection of short stories by Boccaccio.

During the Baroque period, the works of Italian painter, architect, and sculptor Giovanni Lorenzo Bernini (1598–1680), and dramatic religious paintings and portraits by the Venetian artist Titian (1490–1576) were created.

In the twentieth century, new art movements, such as Futurism, were popular in Italy. Twentieth-century Italian poets include Salvatore Quasimodo (1901–1968). Modern Italian novelists include Dario Fo (born 1926); Primo Levi (1919–1987); and Umberto Eco (b. 1932), who wrote *The Name of the Rose*.

◀ Some modern Italian artists draw inspiration from landscapes, while others produce abstract or conceptual art. This artist is working on a classic Italian street scene in Sorrento.

MUSIC AND MOVIES

Italians are justly proud of their musical heritage. Early composers such as Giovanni Palestrina (ca. 1525–1594), Claudio Monteverdi (ca. 1567-1643), and Antonio Vivaldi (ca. 1678–1741) wrote beautiful church music. The nineteenth century was the golden age of Italian opera, with Gioacchino Rossini (1792–1868), Gaetano Donizetti (1797–1848), Giuseppe Verdi (1813–1901), and Giacomo Puccini (1858–1924) all composing great works. Every major Italian city has an opera house. La Scala, in Milan, is the most famous. During the late-twentieth century, the Italian tenor Luciano Pavarotti helped to revive interest in opera worldwide.

Italy is also renowned for filmmaking. An important and influential style of Italian filmmaking was neorealism. During the 1940s, neorealist directors such as Luchino Visconti (1906–1976), Vittorio De Sica (1902–1974), and Roberto Rossellini (1906–1977) made films working in real locations and using local people as well as professional actors. Films such as Visconti's *Ossessione*, De Sica's *The Bicycle Thieves*, and Rossellini's *Stromboli* focused on human problems in natural settings. In the 1960s, "spaghetti Westerns" (so-called because they were made in Italy) became very popular. Italian filmmaker Sergio Leone directed three films, beginning with *A Fistful of Dollars*, which made an international star of American actor Clint Eastwood. Acclaimed Italian film directors of more recent times include Bernardo Bertolucci (b. 1940), who directed *The Last Emperor*, and Roberto Benigni (b. 1952), who directed *Life is Beautiful*.

? Did You Know?

The terms commonly used in written music are Italian. For example, *piano* (soft), *forte* (loud), *lento* (slow), *andante* (moderate walking pace), and *con brio* (lively) are common in musical scores.

▼ An audience settles down for an opera performance at the Roman amphitheater in Verona.

RELIGION

In 1985, a public referendum in Italy decided that Roman Catholicism was no longer to be the country's state religion. Nevertheless, it is still Italy's dominant faith. In 2004, 79.9 percent of Italians were Roman Catholics. About 1.2 percent of Italy's people followed Islam. Most of the country's Muslims were immigrants from North and West Africa. Another 2.3 percent followed other religions, such as Protestantism and Judaism. The remaining 16.6 percent claimed no religion.

In spite of official statistics, the number of practicing Catholics is falling in Italy. About 97 percent of Italians are baptized, but only about one out of three of this group attends church services regularly. Some sources put this figure as low as one in ten. The number of young people entering religious orders has also fallen steeply. Parish priests, however, are respected community members, especially in rural areas, where faith is often stronger than in the cities.

In the past, the Catholic Church exerted great influence on social values in Italy, but, in recent decades, the Church's influence in the country has waned. Catholic doctrine opposes abortion, divorce, and artificial methods of birth control. In 1970, however, Italy's government voted to permit divorce, and Italians voted to legalize abortion in a 1978 referendum. The country's low birth rate suggests that most people in Italy practice birth control.

Focus on: Vatican City

Occupying less than 0.2 sq miles (0.5 sq km) in Rome, Vatican City is the headquarters of the Catholic Church, which has over 850 million followers worldwide. This tiny, independent state has its own diplomatic corps and a security force—the Swiss Guard—with 120 men. Rome has been Catholicism's base ever since St. Peter, the first pope, was buried there in ancient times.

◀ A view of Vatican City and Rome from the roof of St. Peter's Basilica. Vatican City houses masterpieces by Renaissance artists such as Raphael and Michelangelo.

◀ The southern part of the country is the stronghold of Catholicism in Italy. In this picture, the people of Calabria celebrate the feast of the Virgin Mary with a procession.

FESTIVALS

The Church's influence is still strong in terms of tradition and festivals. Most national holidays in Italy are Catholic feast days. In addition to Christmas and Easter, these include Epiphany, All Saints' Day, the Assumption, and the Immaculate Conception. These last two honor the Virgin Mary. Easter is preceded by Lent, a fourty-day period of fasting during which meat is not eaten. Just before Lent, carnivals in Rome, Venice, and elsewhere are held, with people parading through the streets wearing masks and costumes. The word *carnival* comes from the Italian *carne vale*, meaning "meat, farewell."

Towns and villages in Italy each have their own patron saints, whose feast days are celebrated with processions and celebrations. Some of these festivities incorporate customs dating back to medieval or even Roman times. The city of Siena is home to a twice-yearly horse race held to honor the Virgin Mary. In this race, riders in medieval costumes race bareback around Siena's main square.

THE VATICAN

In the eighth century, the Frankish king Charlemagne gave a huge tract of land to the Pope, and this land formed the basis of the Papal States. In addition to ruling this vast territory, popes wielded immense spiritual and political influence. During the 1860s, the papacy opposed Italy's unification, and the Papal States were the last region to become part of Italy in 1870. After the country's unification, popes retreated to Vatican City. In 1929, under Mussolini, the Lateral Treaty formalized relations between Church and state in Italy, and the Vatican became an independent country. In 2005, Pope Benedict XVI became the 264th successor to St. Peter.

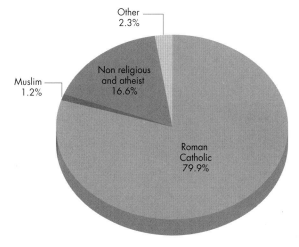

Other
2.3%

Non religious and atheist
16.6%

Muslim
1.2%

Roman Catholic
79.9%

▲ Major religions

CHAPTER 12

Leisure and Tourism

With four to six weeks of paid vacation a year, Italians have more time off than workers in many countries. The country's warm, sunny climate allows Italians to make the most of their leisure time. It also makes Italy a popular destination for foreign tourists.

FAMILY CUSTOMS

The family lies at the heart of Italian culture and everyday life. Traditionally, elderly people have lived with their grown-up children and grandchildren. This practice is becoming less common, especially in big cities, where life is less traditional than in rural areas. In Italian culture, the mother and son are at the center of the family. Many Italian sons remain at home until they reach their thirties, with their mothers attending to their every need. When they marry, however, they may find that their wives are less willing to perform this role because they also go out to work. Italians have a name—*mammismo*—for their national devotion to the idea of the mother. Popular songs are written in praise of mothers.

FOOD

Italian mothers have a reputation for being wonderful cooks. Italians generally are passionate about food, as are many of the visitors to the country who sample real Italian cooking. Italian food is one of the world's most popular cuisines. One of the country's most famous dishes, pizza, is usually eaten as a light meal, followed by a dessert of ice cream, one of Italy's most famous inventions. Italians are

▼ Pizza is baked in an oven in the kitchen of a modern restaurant in Vico Equense, near Naples. In many restaurants in Italy, pizza is still baked in traditional brick-lined ovens.

known for their love of coffee, including different types such as espresso, cappuccino, and caffe latte. Pasta comes in many shapes, including spirals, shells, curls, ribbons, and, of course, spaghetti, or "little strings."

Italians usually buy groceries fresh from the country's many excellent markets. Shops are open in the morning and early evening, but they close between 1 P.M. and 4 P.M. to avoid the hottest part of the day. The main meal in Italy is generally eaten in the evening. It consists of several courses, of which *antipasti,* or appetizers such as cooked meats or salad, are the first. Next is a course of pasta, soup, or risotto, followed by the main dish of meat or fish. The main dish is accompanied or followed by vegetables. Then comes cheese and/or fresh fruit and, finally, dessert. All this may be washed down with a fine Italian wine.

LEISURE ACTIVITIES

Italy's mild climate allows people to spend much of their leisure time outdoors, perhaps enjoying a game of bocce or a drink in the local café. The evening stroll, or *passeggiata*, provides many Italians a chance to gossip with friends and show off new clothes. In towns and cities, Italians enjoy evening concerts and plays, and people from all walks of life—not merely the rich—attend the opera. Italians are also enthusiastic moviegoers, although in recent decades television has caused a drop-off in movie-theater attendance.

Did You Know?

Pasta did not originate in Italy. Marco Polo, the Venetian merchant and traveler, brought it to Italy from China during the thirteenth century.

▼ Onlookers watch the world go by during the evening *passeggiata* in the coastal resort area of Sabaudia, located not far from Rome.

SPORTS

Many Italians love both watching and playing sports, and soccer is often said to be a national obsession. Milan, Turin, and Rome have two major league teams each: Milan is home to AC and Intermilan; Turin is the base for Torino and Juventus; and Roma and Lazio are located in Rome. The national team, nicknamed the *azzurri* (blues), is very popular. Italy has won the World Cup four times, most recently in 2006. In 2006, Italy hosted the Winter Olympics, in Turin.

Cycling has a big following in Italy, with the the *Giro d'Italia* (Tour of Italy) taking place in May or June. Car racing is also popular in Italy. The country has two Formula 1 circuits and is a leading manufacturer of racing cars. Basketball, volleyball, and baseball are played, along with water sports, such as swimming, rowing, and yachting. Many Italians also enjoy skiing and snowboarding in the mountains.

VACATIONS AND TOURISM

Most Italians take at least two weeks of their annual vacation time in the summer, usually in August. At this time, many shops and factories in the country's inland cities close, and traffic jams occur during the mass exodus and return. Over 80 percent of Italians vacation within their own country, heading for the coast or mountains such as the Alps. International travel is becoming increasingly popular in Italy, and more than 26 million Italians traveled abroad as tourists in 2003.

Tourism is an important industry in Italy, bringing in 8.9 percent of the country's foreign earnings in 2003. Tourism also provides employment, although many jobs in hotels, restaurants, and shops are only seasonal. The number of foreign tourists visiting Italy rose in the late 1990s, peaked in 2000, and has dropped off slightly since then. Nearly half of all foreign visitors to Italy head for Venice, and nearly one-quarter of them visit all three of the country's major historic cities of Venice, Rome, and Florence.

◀ In the summer, the mountains of Italy are a magnet both for people on bus tours and for more active visitors such as hikers, climbers, and mountain-bikers.

◀ The famous Leaning Tower of Pisa is now in danger of collapse. Conservation efforts are focused on shoring up the unstable ground on which the tower is built.

Among the many attractions in Italy are art galleries such as the Uffizi, in Florence, and historic sites dating from ancient or Renaissance times, including the Roman town of Pompeii, near Naples; the Greek temples, in Sicily; and the great cathedrals. Coastal resorts such as Portofino, in the northwest; Rimini, on the Adriatic; and Amalfi and Capri, further south, are popular with Italians and foreigners. While vital to the economy, tourism also causes problems, including traffic congestion and pollution. Uncontrolled development has spoiled some stretches of the Italian coast.

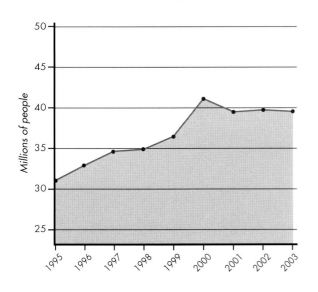

▲ Changes in international tourism, 1990–2003

Tourism in Italy

- 🗁 Tourist arrivals, millions: 39.604
- 🗁 Earnings from tourism in U.S.$: 32,565,999,616
- 🗁 Tourism as % foreign earnings: 8.9
- 🗁 Tourist departures, millions: 26.817
- 🗁 Expenditure on tourism in U.S.$: 23,723,999,232

Source: World Bank

 Did You Know?

The Leaning Tower of Pisa is a major tourist attraction. Subsidence caused the tower to lean soon after its construction began in 1173.

CHAPTER 13

Environment and Conservation

Land, air, and water pollution are all problems in Italy, especially in densely populated and highly industrialized areas. Wild habitats are disappearing. Although national parks help to protect Italy's wildlife, some of its species are under threat.

AIR AND WATER POLLUTION

In built-up areas, exhaust from traffic and emissions from industry cause air pollution. Cities such as Bologna and Milan have closed some of their central areas to traffic in an effort to curb pollution and congestion, while Naples and Florence have introduced buses that run on cleaner fuels, such as liquified petroleum gas (LPG). Waste gases from cars, cities, and power stations mix with water vapor in the air to produce acid rain, which damages historic buildings. Acid rain also kills trees and wildlife in lakes and rivers. It is a particular problem in the country's northern industrial areas. Since the 1980s, the government has introduced laws to curb the release of waste gases.

As a highly industrialized nation, Italy burns large amounts of fossil fuels, adding to the release of carbon dioxide (CO_2) and other gases that contribute to global warming. Warming weather worldwide is causing rising sea levels, which may threaten low-lying cities, such as Venice, in the future. Italy has signed the Kyoto Protocol, an international agreement to reduce

▼ This electric car, made by the Italian company Start Lab, helps to improve urban environments. Its small size eases congestion and parking difficulties.

CO$_2$ emissions, and its government has set targets for reducing emissions.

Italy's rivers and surrounding seas are polluted by waste from towns, factories, and agriculture. The Mediterranean is one of the world's most polluted seas, and the Adriatic Sea is one of the worst affected areas. Pesticides and fertilizers used in farming run off the land into rivers such as the Po and discharge into coastal waters, causing algae to multiply. This so-called algae bloom reduces oxygen levels in the water, harming aquatic life. It is also unsightly and smelly, which discourages tourists. Italy participates in several treaties that restrict the dumping of waste at sea, but agricultural run-off is difficult to regulate.

Focus on: Venice in Peril

The city of Venice is under threat. Its historic buildings are slowly but surely sinking into the lagoon in which the city is located. Pollutants in seawater are eating away at the foundations of its buildings, and the buildings are also damaged by the waves caused by passing boats. In winter, when very high tides occur, seawater floods parts of the city, including St. Mark's Square, which features ancient and beautiful buildings. The worst floods in Venice have occurred in 1966, 1979, and 1986. Many solutions to this problem have been proposed. The most practical of these may be to build a barrier across the lagoon entrances to protect against very high tides.

▲ Tourists wade barefoot across a flooded St. Mark's Square, in Venice, after fall rains and high tides caused the water level of the Venetian lagoon to rise.

THREATS TO LAND AND SOIL

In the past, Italy disposed of huge amounts of domestic waste in pits called landfill sites. Now, a shortage of such sites is causing a crisis in waste disposal in the country. Italy's government encourages recycling to reduce the amount of waste. Italy's record on recycling is one of the best in the world. About half of its used paper and glass is recycled.

Over the last 2,000 years, most of the ancient forests that once covered Italy have been felled. Without the roots of trees and other plants to

▼ An Italian woman in Naples recycles used glass bottles. Recycling centers like this one are now in use all over Italy.

keep the soil in place, the land quickly erodes. Deforestation and overgrazing by livestock have led to erosion on steep hillsides. In 1996, a landslide into the Bay of Naples damaged property and killed five people. One way to fight erosion is to plant more trees. Much of the 23 percent of Italy that is covered by forests has been fairly recently planted. Another way to limit erosion is to reduce the amount of livestock grazing in steep areas.

In general, wetlands absorb moisture and help prevent flooding. Draining of wetlands to create new land for industry and farming has increased the risk of floods in Italy. In 1966, priceless artworks in Florence were ruined when the River Arno burst its banks. The worst floods in Italy in recent decades struck Piedmont and Liguria in 1994.

WILDLIFE AND CONSERVATION

Italy's spectacular wildlife includes golden eagles, bears, wolves, and lynx in the country's remote mountains, as well as wild boar and mouflon sheep (a type of wild mountain sheep) on Sardinia. Italy's wildlife is under threat for several reasons, of which habitat loss is the most important. Over the centuries, grasslands, forests, marshes, and even remote uplands have been cleared to make space for new farms, industrial sites, roads, and suburbs. Very little natural vegetation is left in areas such as the Po Valley.

Mammals such as deer and boars are threatened by many Italians' enthusiasm for hunting, as are songbirds. Italy's hunting lobby is a powerful force in the country. In a 1990 referendum, it won the vote against a ban on hunting. Although hunting is legal, laws protect endangered species such as wolves, bears, and boars. The setting up of reserves and national parks has helped to preserve some rare species. Italy has about twenty national parks, some of which date from the 1920s, and more are planned. Alpine parks such as Stelvio and Gran Paradiso protect chamois, a type of goat antelope; ibex, a type of wild goat; and marmots, or ground squirrels. Mouflon sheep and boars roam in Sardinian reserves.

Environmental and Conservation Data

📁 Forested area as % total land area: 23.7

📁 Protected area as % total land area: 7.6

📁 Number of protected areas: 11,141

SPECIES DIVERSITY

Category	Known species	Threatened species
Mammals	269	45
Breeding birds	528	38
Reptiles	94	6
Amphibians	32	n/a
Fish	199	13
Plants	11,400	7

Source: World Resources Institute

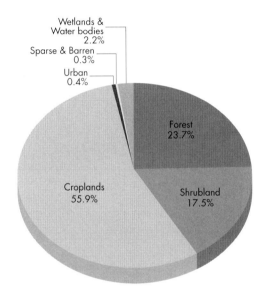

Wetlands & Water bodies 2.2%

Sparse & Barren 0.3%

Urban 0.4%

Forest 23.7%

Croplands 55.9%

Shrubland 17.5%

▲ Habitat type as percentage of total area

? Did You Know?

Stelvio, which is located in the Alps of Lombardy, is Italy's largest national park, covering 521 sq miles (1,350 sq km).

◀ Pony trekking is an environmentally friendly way to see the landscape of Italy's Abruzzo National Park.

CHAPTER 14

Future Challenges

Italy entered the twenty-first century as a dynamic, prosperous nation with a well-developed economy. Italy's generous welfare system allows most of its people to enjoy a good quality of life. However, persistent problems remain, including sluggish economic growth, organized crime, and the divide between the northern and southern parts of the country.

DIVISIONS WITHIN ITALY

In spite of the funds spent on southern Italy since the 1950s, the country still divides into a prosperous north and a welfare-dependent south with high unemployment. Much has been done to generate industry and improve the infrastructure in the south, but southern Italy's natural disadvantages remain. The government cannot change the harsh southern climate, which makes farming difficult, nor can it remedy the scarcity of resources. Future governments of Italy will need to try to continue supporting the south while placating the Northern League—a difficult balancing act.

The political scandals of the 1990s caused a major shake-up in Italian politics but did little to reduce the country's bureaucracy, which stifles political and economic reform. Recent prime ministers have been elected on pledges to root out the Mafia and other criminal groups. Yet the Mafia's octopus-like tentacles continue to reach all levels of Italian society.

▼ The wealth of northern Italy is reflected in this shopping center in Milan.

 Poverty is still a persistent problem in many parts of southern Italy, including on the island of Sardinia. Poorer people, including members of ethnic minorities such as the Roma (shown here), often struggle to survive.

WELFARE AND THE ECONOMY

Many analysts predict that Italy's population will fall within the next few decades. If current trends continue, the country's population may drop from 57 million to around 40 million by 2050. The growing numbers of older people will place an increasing burden on the country in terms of pensions, medical care, and other benefits. The government recently reduced its financial commitments by changing the rules on pensions, including those of government employees. Government employees used to be able to retire after 25 years of employment. This has been raised to 35 years, with a retirement age of 57. Meanwhile, to help pay for its welfare system, the government could gain additional contributions towards its Gross National Product if it were to succeed in taxing those who operate within the informal, or "hidden," economy.

Since the late 1950s, Italy has been at the forefront of European politics. Many Italians believe the European Union has had a positive effect on the country's economy, helping to tighten monetary policy and stimulate new growth. Many Italians also look to the EU to reduce unemployment and keep inflation rates low. In recent decades, Italy has struggled with its balance of payments, with spending on imports exceeding the revenue from exports. Future governments of Italy will continue the effort to stimulate economic growth while considering the needs of the country's environment—another delicate balancing act.

? Did You Know?

Italy currently spends about 10 percent of its Gross National Product on pensions—more than double the amount it spends on education.

Time Line

800–900 B.C. The Phoenicians colonize parts of southern Italy.

700–800 B.C. The Greeks found colonies in southern Italy.

600–700 B.C. The Etruscan civilization reaches its height in central Italy.

509 B.C. Etruscans are driven out of Rome by a Latin-speaking tribe, and Rome becomes a republic.

27 B.C.–A.D. 14 Augustus rules as the first Roman emperor.

A.D. 79 An eruption of Vesuvius destroys the Roman town of Pompeii.

117 The Roman Empire reaches its greatest extent, under the Emperor Trajan.

264 The start of the reign of Emperor Diocletian, during which the Roman Empire is divided into eastern and western halves.

330 Emperor Constantine moves capital of Roman Empire to Byzantium (now Istanbul).

476 Barbarian leader Odoacer sacks Rome and deposes the last western Roman emperor. The eastern branch, the Byzantine Empire, remains intact.

800 Land given to the pope by Frankish king Charlemagne forms the basis of the Papal States. Charlemagne is crowned emperor of the Romans by the pope. This allegiance forms the basis for the Holy Roman Empire.

800–1100 Holy Roman emperors vie with successive popes for control of northern Italy. This rivalry allows for the emergence of the Italian city-states.

1000s The Normans colonize Sicily and southern Italy.

1265 The French become rulers of Sicily.

1300–1550 The age of the Renaissance.

c.1520–1550 Spain and the Holy Roman Empire defeat France to control much of Italy.

1633 Italian astronomer Galileo Galilei is tried by the Inquisition.

1707 Austrian rulers take control of northern Italy.

1797 French emperor Napoleon Bonaparte invades northern Italy, bringing the ideals of the French Revolution. He founds several republics.

1815 Napoleon is defeated, and Italy is returned to its former rulers, including Austria and Spain.

1859–1860 Piedmontese forces under Count Cavour defeat the Austrians in northern Italy and head south. Garibaldi and a force of 1,000 soldiers land in Sicily and move north to meet the Piedmontese army at Teano.

1861 The kingdom of Italy is proclaimed under the ruler of Piedmont-Sardinia, King Victor Emanuel II.

1866 Venice becomes part of the kingdom of Italy.

1870 The Papal States become part of Italy.

1908 A major earthquake strikes the port of Messina in Sicily, killing about 70,000 people.

1911 Italy seizes Libya in North Africa.

1915–1918 Italy sides with the Allies (Britain, France, and Russia) during World War I.

1922 Fascist leader Benito Mussolini becomes prime minister.

1925 Mussolini becomes dictator of Italy.

1936 Italy seizes control of Ethiopia.

1940 Under Mussolini, Italy enters World War II on the side of Germany.

1945 War in Europe ends in victory for the Allies.

1946 Italy votes to abolish the monarchy and become a republic.

1948 Italy's new constitution comes into effect. Christian Democrats form the first of many coalition governments.

1950s Italy industrializes rapidly.

1950–1984 Italian governments fund the *Cassa per il Mezzogiorno* to develop southern Italy.

1957 Italy becomes one of six nations to found the European Economic Community (EEC), which later becomes the European Union (EU).

1966 The River Arno floods in Florence, damaging art treasures. Venice also floods.

1970 Divorce is made legal in Italy.

1973–1980 The rise of terrorism in Italy by both right- and left-wing extremist groups.

1978 The Red Brigades kidnap and assassinate ex-prime minister Aldo Moro. Italians vote to make abortion legal. The election of the Polish cardinal who became Pope John Paul II breaks 400 years of tradition, during which all popes had been Italian.

1980 An earthquake in Campania in southern Italy kills more than 4,500 people.

1983 Bettino Craxi becomes Italy's first socialist prime minister.

1985 Roman Catholicism ceases to be Italy's state religion.

1987 A mass trial of Mafia suspects in Palermo results in 338 convictions.

1990 The Northern League, a political party, emerges, calling for northern Italy to become independent of the south.

1992 Sicilian judge Giovanni Falcone is killed by a Mafia car bomb.

1992–1993 The *Tangentopoli* political scandals bring about the downfall of many leading politicians and existing parties, such as the Christian Democrats. Birth of new political alliances.

1993 The EEC becomes the European Union (EU) with fifteen members.

1994 A coalition including *Forza Italia* led by Silvio Berlusconi takes power. However, Berlusconi resigns following accusations of corruption later the same year.

1994 Floods in northwest Italy kill more than 100 people.

1996 The Olive Tree Alliance takes power in Italy.

2001 Silvio Berlusconi is re-elected prime minister.

2002 Italy adopts the euro.

2005 Pope Benedict XVI became the 264th successor to St. Peter.

September 2005 Italy seeks help from the EU to deal with the large numbers of illegal immigrants attempting to enter the country.

April 2006 A center-left coalition led by Romano Prodi takes power after a narrow victory.

Glossary

Allies the name given to the combined forces fighting against the German side during the two world wars; in World War I, Britain, France, Italy, Russia, and the United States fought against Germany, Austria-Hungary, and Turkey; in World War II, Britain, France, the United States, and the Soviet Union were allied against Germany, Italy, and Japan

coalition a government formed by an alliance between several political parties

Communist Party a political party advocating communism, a system of government in which power resides with a single party that controls all economic activity and provides services

conservative having an outlook that opposes rapid change; in party politics, a right-wing party that supports private ownership

constitution a set of laws governing a country or organization

democracy a political system in which government leaders are chosen by people voting in free elections

depose to overthrow

developed countries the richer countries of the world that have well-developed industries, including the United States, many European nations, and Japan

dictator a ruler with absolute (complete) authority

erosion the wearing away of the land by natural forces, such as wind, rain, and ice; erosion is sometimes caused by deforestation

exodus a mass departure

Fascist in politics, a party that favors strict government control of labor and industry and often promotes the importance of nation and/or race over individual people

fossil fuel fuels such as coal, oil, and gas, that formed from fossilized remains of plants or animals that lived millions of years ago

Frankish having to do with the Franks, a Germanic nation that conquered France in the sixth century

fresco a mural painting in which pigment (paint) is applied directly to wet plaster

geothermal energy energy from hot rocks located underground

global warming worldwide rising temperatures caused by the increase of carbon dioxide and other gases in the atmosphere that trap the Sun's heat

industrialization the process of developing a country's industries and manufacturing

inflation a general increase in prices of goods

infrastructure the basic facilities needed for a country to function, including communications and transportation

Internet host an Internet site often representing an organization and ending in .com, .net or .org

irrigation the watering of land by artificial means in order to grow crops

liberal in general, not bound by traditional ways; in politics, having to do with political parties that support broad reforms and the use of government to distribute wealth

literacy the ability to read and write

North Atlantic Treaty Organization (NATO) a military alliance formed between the United States and several European countries after World War II in order to help prevent a Soviet invasion of Europe

papacy the office of the pope, who is the head of the Roman Catholic Church

papal having to do with the pope

partisan a member of a resistance group that is loyal to and fights for a particular side in a conflict

pollutant a substance that dirties the air, water, or land when released

proportional representation a system of electing members of parliament by giving seats to political parties according to their share of the vote in the whole country

puppet state a country that is controlled by another but has its own ruler who has little real power

quota a share allotted by agreement to a particular organization or country

reactor the part of a nuclear power plant where energy is made by splitting atoms

referendum a public vote on a single issue

republic a nation-state without a monarch that is ruled by the people through their elected representatives

Risorgimento the movement to unify Italy in the 1800s; "resurrection" in Italian

sewage dirty water that carries chemicals and human waste from homes and factories

socialist having to do with a person or a political movement favoring a system of government in which a nation's means of production are owned and run by the government

subsidence the sinking of the ground level

tectonic plate one of the giant rigid sections that make up Earth's outer layer or crust

toll a fee charged for use of a road or other transportation link

turbine a machine powered by steam, gas, or water that is used to generate electricity

United Nations (UN) an organization founded at the end of World War II with the aim of enabling diplomacy, solving international problems, and preventing future wars

Further Information

BOOKS TO READ

Barber, Nicola. *Rome* (Great Cities of the World). World Almanac Library, 2004.

Bastable, Tony. *John Cabot* (Great Explorers). World Almanac Library, 2004.

Collier, Martin. *Italian Unification 1820-71* (Heinemann Advanced History). Heinemann Educational, 2003.

Connolly, Sean. *Botticelli* (Lives of the Artists). World Almanac Library, 2005.

Deem, James. *Bodies from the Ash: Life and Death in Ancient Pompeii.* Houghton Mifflin, 2005.

Garrington, Sally. *Italy* (Countries of the World). Facts on File, 2004.

Gefen, Keren. *Marco Polo* (Great Explorers) World Almanac Library, 2002.

Mason, Antony. *Leonardo da Vinci* (Lives of the Artists). World Almanac Library, 2004.

Nesbitt (editor), Mark R. *Living in Renaissance Italy* (Exploring Cultural History). Greenhaven Press, 2005.

Roberts, Jeremy. *Benito Mussolini* (A&E Biography). Lerner Publishing Group, 2005.

Sadik, Ademola. *Italy* (The European Union: Political, Social, and Economic Cooperation). Mason Crest Publishers, 2005.

Steele, Philip. *Galileo: The Genius Who Faced the Inquisition* World History Biographies). National Geographic Children's Books, 2005.

USEFUL WEB SITES

CIA World Factbook: Italy
www.cia.gov/cia/publications/factbook/geos/it.html

Getty Exhibitions: Italy on the Grand Tour
www.getty.edu/art/exhibitions/grand_tour/

Italian State Tourist Board
www.italiantouristboard.co.uk/

Time for Kids: Italy Wins World Cup
www.timeforkids.com/TFK/news/story/0,6260,1212216,00.html

Torino 2006
www.torino2006.org/ENG/OlympicGames/home/

Vesuvius, Italy
volcano.und.nodak.edu/vwdocs/volc_images/europe_west_asia/vesuvius_more/vesuvius_more.html

Publisher's note to educators and parents: Our editors have carefully reviewed these Web sites to ensure that they are suitable for children. Many Web sites change frequently, however, and we cannot guarantee that a site's future contents will continue to meet our high standards of quality and educational value. Be advised that children should be closely supervised whenever they access the Internet.

Index

Page numbers in **bold** indicate pictures.

About the Author

Dr. Jen Green received a doctorate from the University of Sussex (Department of English and American Studies) in 1982. She worked in publishing for fifteen years and is now a full-time writer who has written more than 150 books for children. She lives in England.